How to Draw
Bugs

Written by Michelle Petty
Illustrated by Janice Kinnealy

Copyright © 1997 by Troll Communications L.L.C. All rights reserved.
Printed in the United States of America. ISBN 0-8167-4447-5
10 9 8 7 6 5 4 3 2

Materials Needed

The following materials will be helpful to you as you learn to draw all your favorite creepy, crawly critters!

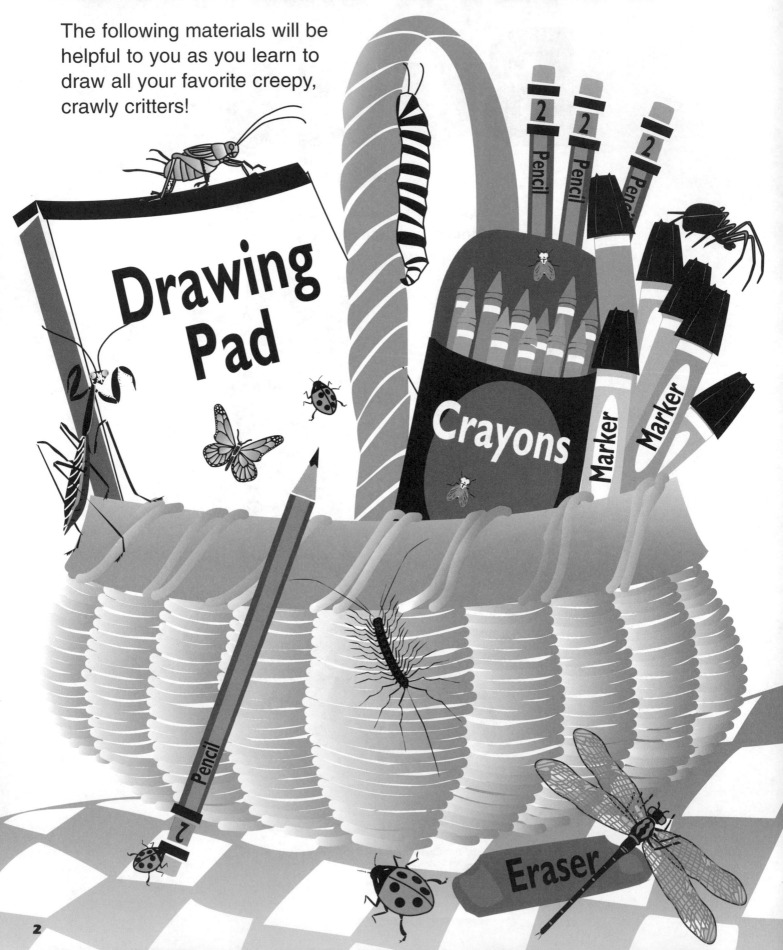

Introduction

Welcome to the world of insects! It is a world of amazing creatures that perform incredible tasks. As you learn to draw the many insects in this book you will learn where each one lives, what it eats, and some interesting facts that make each insect unique.

Each of the drawings in this book is shown in several simple steps. Begin with a pencil and follow each step, adding to your drawing as you go along. When your drawing looks the way you want it to, color it with crayons, markers, colored pencils, or whatever you want!

Remember, the best part of your drawing is what *you* add to it with a little imagination. Show a black widow spider in its web waiting to attack. Draw a large group of ants working together in an ant community. Or maybe a grasshopper about to jump from one blade of grass to another. The possibilities are endless—just as your imagination is endless. So, sharpen your pencil and get ready to draw bugs!

Caterpillar

Caterpillars are long and wriggly and come in all colors and sizes. The caterpillar's body is designed to protect it from birds, who love to eat caterpillars. Some caterpillars are brightly colored to warn birds that they taste bad. And some are the same colors as the plants they live on so they can hide on the plant. When a caterpillar is all grown up it surrounds itself with a protective coating called a *pupa*. Inside the pupa there are magic changes taking place. In a few months, the pupa opens and a butterfly comes out!

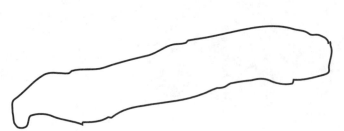

1. Draw a long, bumpy worm shape as shown, making the head wider than the tail.

2. Draw thick stripes on the caterpillar's body with a heavy stroke. Add two thin antennae at the head.

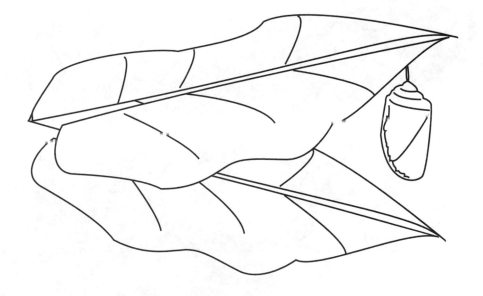

1. To draw the caterpillar's pupa, start with a small plump oval shape. The caterpillar's body is curled up inside the pupa.

2. The pupa hangs from a leaf. Sketch in two large leaves. Fill in detail on the pupa, putting curved lines at the top and making it slightly narrower as shown.

Butterfly

Butterflies can often be found sitting on a flower. Do you know what the butterfly is doing? It is using its long hollow tongue to suck a sweet liquid called *nectar* from the flower—just like drinking through a straw! Some of these beautiful, delicate insects have special designs on their wings that look like eyes. When a bird is about to attack, the butterfly opens its wings to show the "eyes." This scares away the bird or tricks it into attacking the "eyes" instead of the butterfly's body.

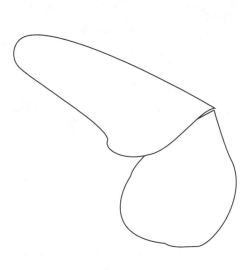

1. Draw one pair of the butterfly's wings. Each one is like a leaf shape. Use careful, sloping lines and make the wings just touch each other as shown.

2. Make a small, circular head with two long, skinny ovals underneath it as shown. Put in two more wings exactly like the first two.

3. Now add two small antennae and two longer, graceful ones at the head. Carefully draw designs on your butterfly's wings. You can be as detailed as you want but keep both sides *symmetrical*, or the exact mirror image of each other.

Ant

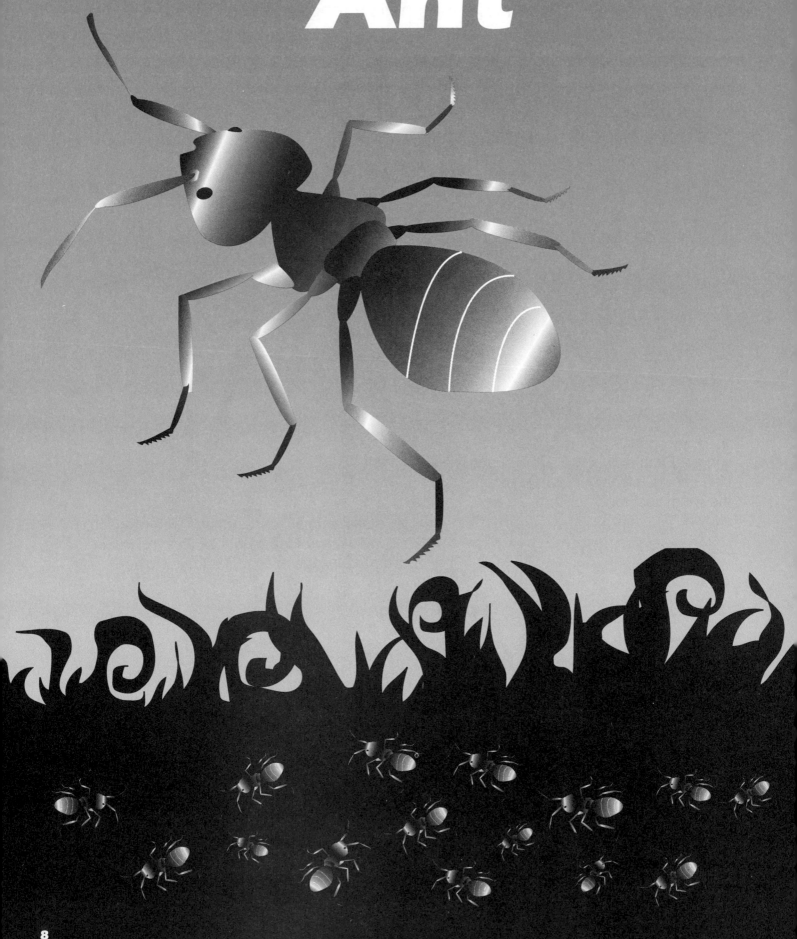

An **ant** is part of the insect group called "true bugs." True bugs eat through a feeding tube rather than chewing food up as beetles do. Ants live in large underground communities where each ant has a special job. Some are soldiers who defend the ants' home. Some are nurses who care for baby ants. Some are in charge of gathering food while others build new places to live. Ants are good at working together. They "talk" to each other by tapping each other with their *antennae*, or feelers.

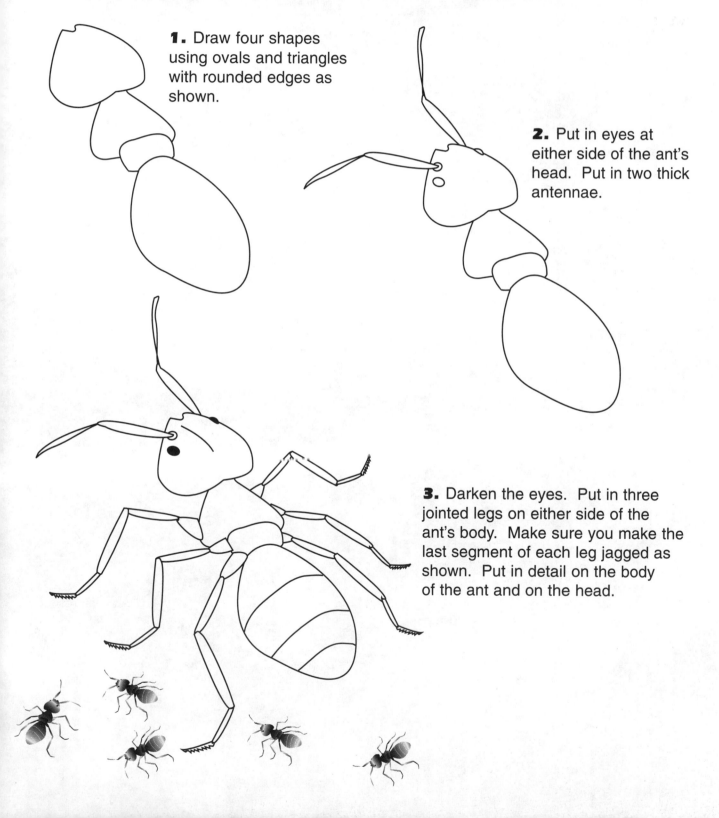

1. Draw four shapes using ovals and triangles with rounded edges as shown.

2. Put in eyes at either side of the ant's head. Put in two thick antennae.

3. Darken the eyes. Put in three jointed legs on either side of the ant's body. Make sure you make the last segment of each leg jagged as shown. Put in detail on the body of the ant and on the head.

Ladybug

Ladybugs are a type of beetle. Ladybugs are very helpful to people. They eat so many pests that farmers sometimes use them instead of chemicals to control insects that harm crops. Ladybugs, like all beetles, have hard outer wings to protect them and strong jaws for chewing. Underneath their hard shell, ladybugs have soft wings for flying. In the winter, ladybugs hibernate!

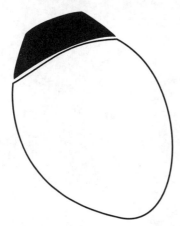

1. Start out by sketching an oval shape. Top it off with a solid black area as shown.

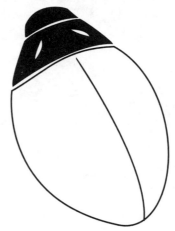

2. Add a solid dome-shaped head at the top. Give your ladybug two slanted slots on its back by erasing carefully as shown. Touch it up with a sharp pencil point.

3. Now add antennae and spots—put the spots in any pattern you like. Each spot can be a slightly different shape and size—they don't have to be perfect circles.

4. Finally, give your ladybug legs—three on each side. Make the legs jointed as shown.

Centipede

Some **centipedes** have about 30 legs while others have as many as 200! They run very fast and eat slugs and other pests, catching them with their poisoned claws. They even chase earthworms right into their homes and eat them! **Millipedes** have more legs than centipedes. However, a millipede moves slower than a centipede because it feeds on old leaves and rotting wood and doesn't need to rush to catch its food. If a millipede is frightened, it squirts a smelly liquid to keep birds and frogs away. Even so, some birds and frogs still like to eat them.

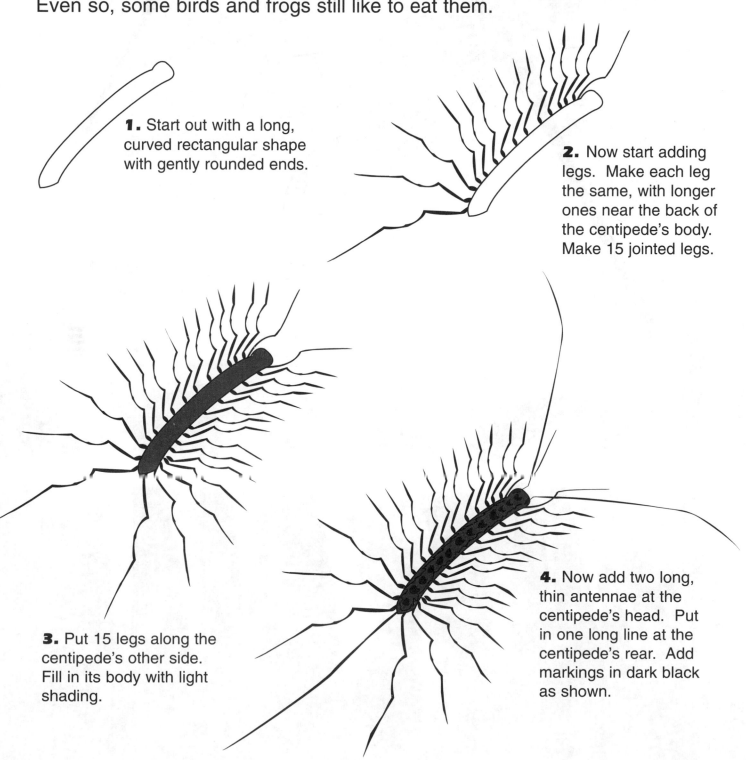

1. Start out with a long, curved rectangular shape with gently rounded ends.

2. Now start adding legs. Make each leg the same, with longer ones near the back of the centipede's body. Make 15 jointed legs.

3. Put 15 legs along the centipede's other side. Fill in its body with light shading.

4. Now add two long, thin antennae at the centipede's head. Put in one long line at the centipede's rear. Add markings in dark black as shown.

Dragonfly

A **dragonfly** can fly very fast—up to 56 miles (90 km) per hour. Dragonflies catch other insects while flying by holding their legs underneath their bodies like a basket and scooping up the unlucky insect as it passes. They have a very powerful *compound eye* that is made up of many lenses. This eye helps the dragonfly spot other insects from far away. Dragonflies can be helpful to us because they catch thousands of pesky mosquitoes. Dragonflies like to fly around calm bodies of water like a lake or pond, but they can be found in forests as well.

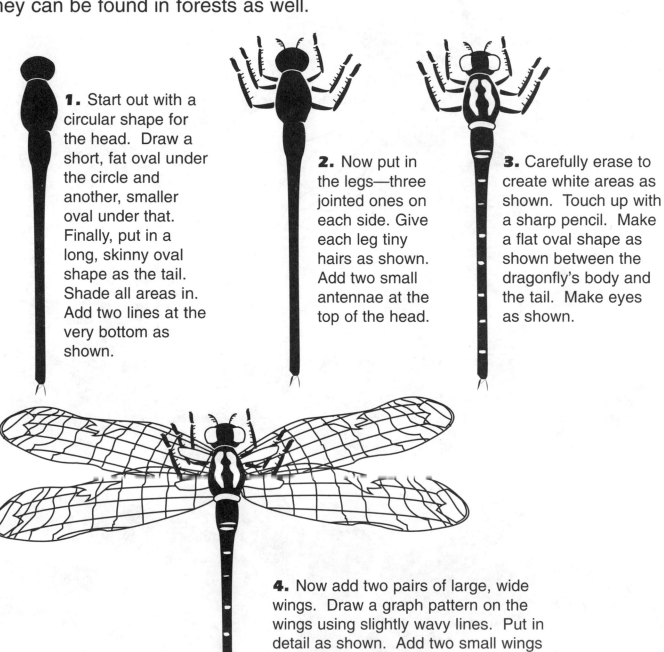

1. Start out with a circular shape for the head. Draw a short, fat oval under the circle and another, smaller oval under that. Finally, put in a long, skinny oval shape as the tail. Shade all areas in. Add two lines at the very bottom as shown.

2. Now put in the legs—three jointed ones on each side. Give each leg tiny hairs as shown. Add two small antennae at the top of the head.

3. Carefully erase to create white areas as shown. Touch up with a sharp pencil. Make a flat oval shape as shown between the dragonfly's body and the tail. Make eyes as shown.

4. Now add two pairs of large, wide wings. Draw a graph pattern on the wings using slightly wavy lines. Put in detail as shown. Add two small wings on either side of the dragonfly's body. Carefully erase unwanted lines.

Bumblebee

How do **bumblebees** help flowers grow? They like to drink nectar that is inside the flowers. As they crawl on the flower, a powder called *pollen* sticks to their bodies. The bees spread pollen from one flower to another as they eat nectar. This is important because plants need pollen to form new flowers. Bumblebees live in big groups. They have a queen in charge of all of them. The bees all work together to take care of the queen.

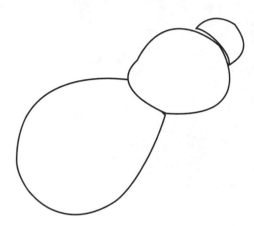

1. Draw two circular shapes with a half-circle at the top as shown—sort of like a snowman lying down!

2. Fill in detail around the edges of the two larger circles, adding stripes in as shown. Fill in the small half circle and add two curved antennae.

3. Put in three jointed legs on either side of the middle circle. Draw in oval-shaped eyes on either side of the bee's head, just underneath the antennae.

4. Now add the wings by sketching in long pear shapes on either side of the middle circle. Erase unwanted lines and sketch in detail on the wings as shown.

Housefly

Ever wish you could walk up walls and onto the ceiling? Well, a **housefly** can. Like most flies, the housefly has very special feet. The bottom of a fly's foot is covered with sticky, hairy pads. These pads keep the fly from falling off the ceiling or sliding down a wall. A fly has special eyes, too. Its eyes are so big, they cover almost all of the fly's head. Each eye is made up of about 4,000 lenses. That's why flies are so hard to catch—they can see even the slightest movement from anywhere in a room.

1. Draw four stacked shapes as shown to make the fly's head and body.

2. Sketch in the fly's big eyes. They should take up almost the whole head. Shade all portions in, leaving thin lines as detail. Put in the antennae as shown.

3. Now add three jointed legs on either side. Make sure the feet have small hairs on them. Now the fly can walk up walls!

4. Lightly sketch the fly's delicate wings as shown. Put thin lines through each wing but don't erase anything—the fly's wings are supposed to be see-through.

Mosquito

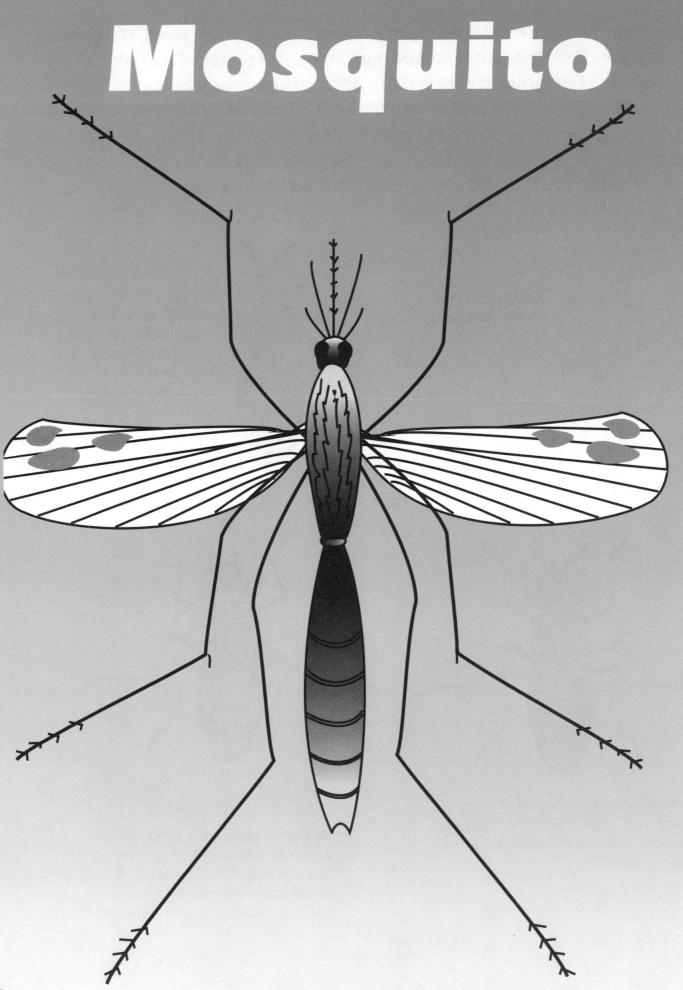

Did you know that only the female **mosquito** bites? When she bites you, she stabs your skin with a needle-like part of her mouth called a stinger. She injects her saliva into you while she drinks. Her saliva is what causes the bite to swell up and get itchy. Mosquitoes can be very pesky but they can also be dangerous. In some parts of the world, mosquitoes can spread very serious diseases.

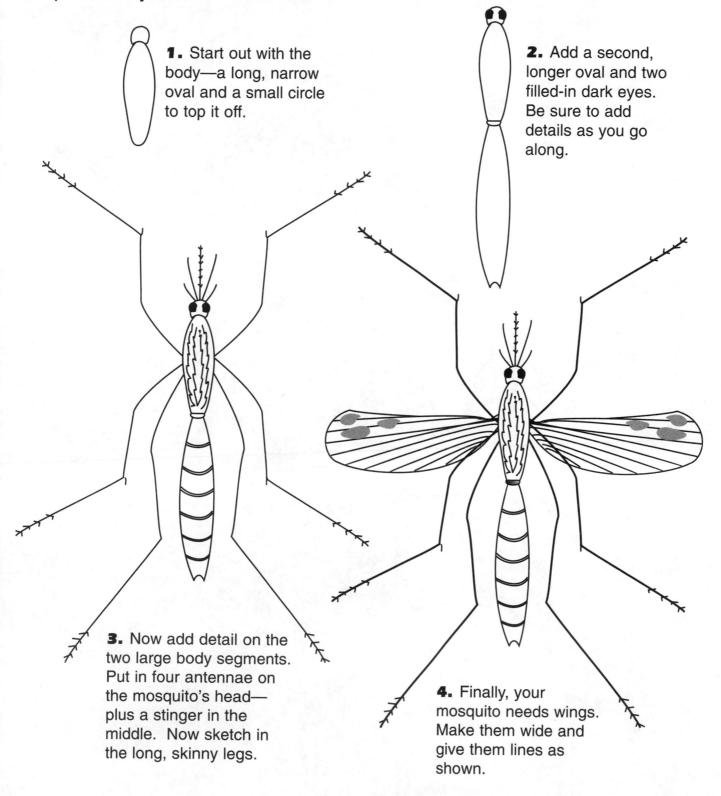

1. Start out with the body—a long, narrow oval and a small circle to top it off.

2. Add a second, longer oval and two filled-in dark eyes. Be sure to add details as you go along.

3. Now add detail on the two large body segments. Put in four antennae on the mosquito's head— plus a stinger in the middle. Now sketch in the long, skinny legs.

4. Finally, your mosquito needs wings. Make them wide and give them lines as shown.

Firefly

A **firefly** is not really a fly—it's a soft-bodied beetle. The end of a firefly, or lightning bug, lights up when air is let in through special tubes in its body. Some countries that don't have electricity use jars of fireflies as lamps. Each firefly blinks its light in a special pattern that is different from any other firefly.

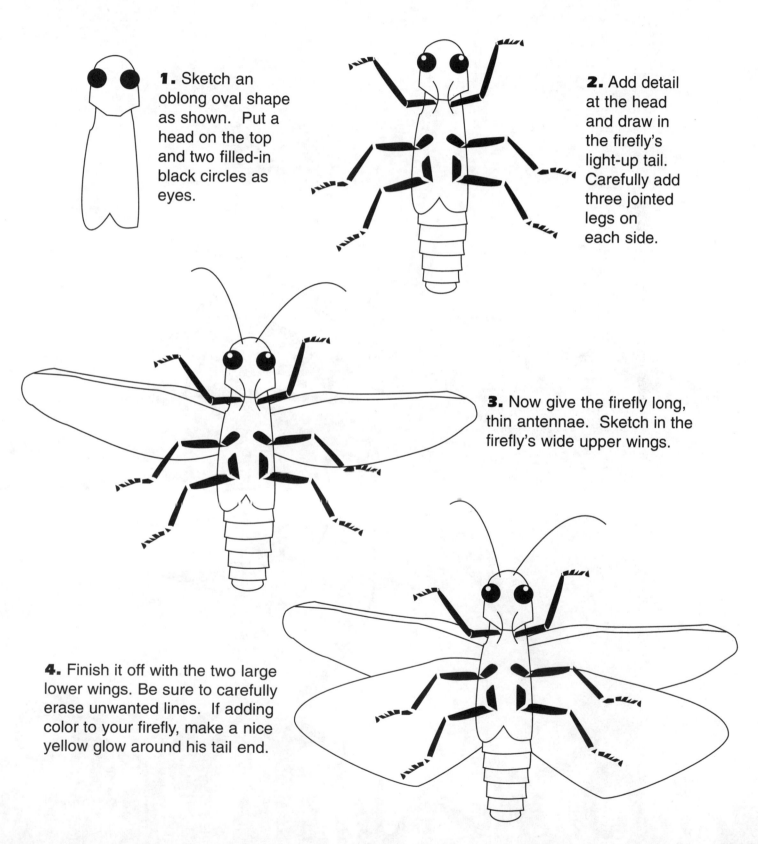

1. Sketch an oblong oval shape as shown. Put a head on the top and two filled-in black circles as eyes.

2. Add detail at the head and draw in the firefly's light-up tail. Carefully add three jointed legs on each side.

3. Now give the firefly long, thin antennae. Sketch in the firefly's wide upper wings.

4. Finish it off with the two large lower wings. Be sure to carefully erase unwanted lines. If adding color to your firefly, make a nice yellow glow around his tail end.

Jumping Spider

The **jumping spider** jumps on insects to eat them instead of catching them in a web like other spiders. The jumping spider is very colorful and has lots of bright fringes of hair decorating its legs and body. Jumping spiders anchor themselves with a string of web when they are getting ready to jump. That way, if they miss their target, they will be anchored and won't fall.

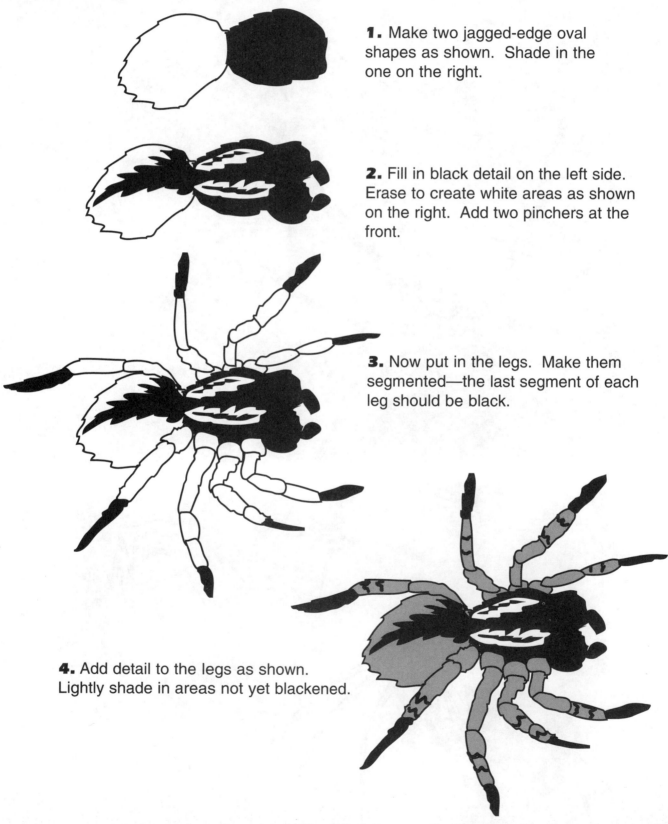

1. Make two jagged-edge oval shapes as shown. Shade in the one on the right.

2. Fill in black detail on the left side. Erase to create white areas as shown on the right. Add two pinchers at the front.

3. Now put in the legs. Make them segmented—the last segment of each leg should be black.

4. Add detail to the legs as shown. Lightly shade in areas not yet blackened.

Black Widow Spider

There are several types of **black widow spider** living in North America and they are all poisonous. The male is much smaller than the female and does not bite. The black widow is small, roundish, and inky black. Black widows are marked with a red or yellow hourglass shape. The bite of a black widow spider will not kill a person but will cause severe stomach pains. There is medicine available to fight the effect of the spider's *venom*, or poison. If you are bitten by a black widow, see a doctor right away.

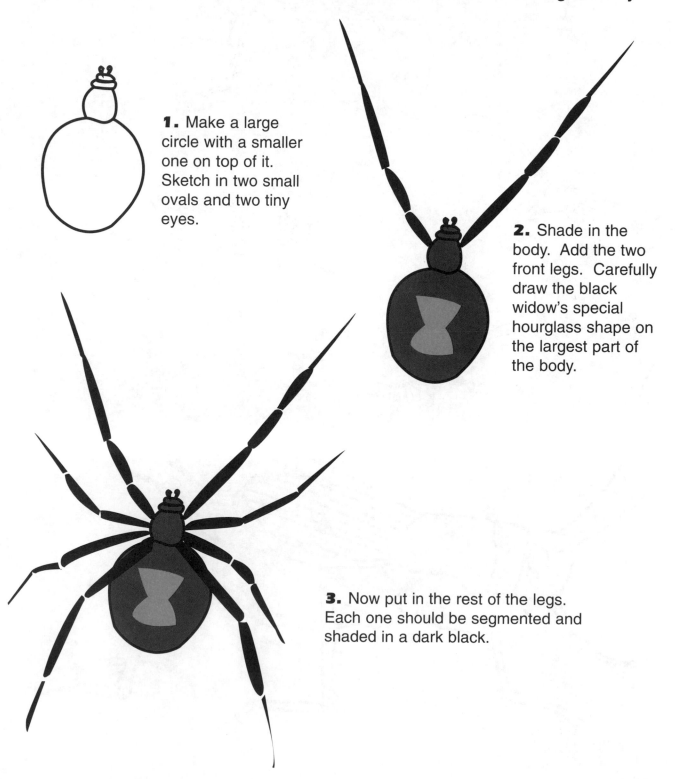

1. Make a large circle with a smaller one on top of it. Sketch in two small ovals and two tiny eyes.

2. Shade in the body. Add the two front legs. Carefully draw the black widow's special hourglass shape on the largest part of the body.

3. Now put in the rest of the legs. Each one should be segmented and shaded in a dark black.

Cricket

Have you ever heard a **cricket** "sing" at night in summertime? Only male crickets can make this singing noise, which is actually the sound made by his wings rubbing together. This chirping noise sounds like singing. Most crickets like to live in fields, where they eat grass and other plants. Sometimes the cricket will eat other insects as well. Every now and then, a cricket will wind up in your house. Some people think having a cricket in the house is good luck!

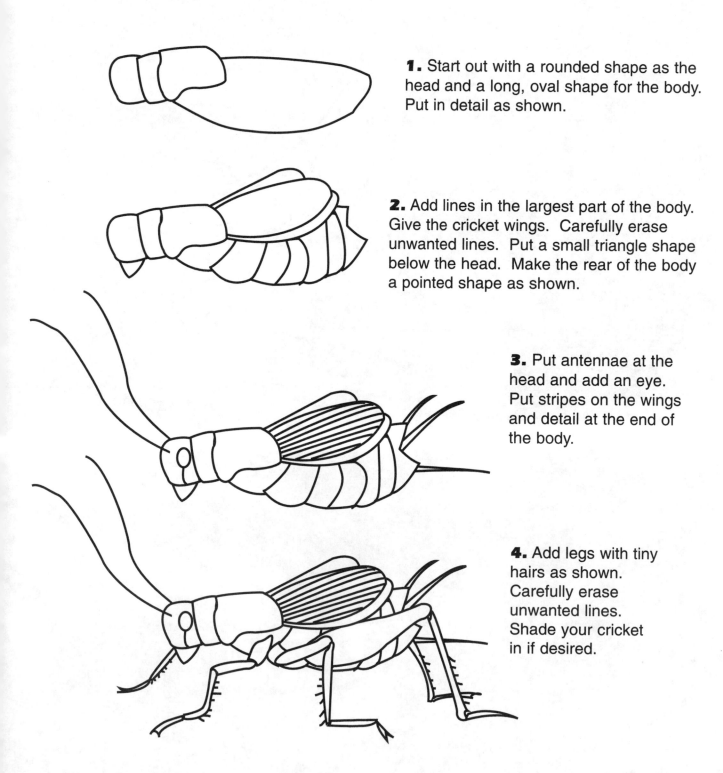

1. Start out with a rounded shape as the head and a long, oval shape for the body. Put in detail as shown.

2. Add lines in the largest part of the body. Give the cricket wings. Carefully erase unwanted lines. Put a small triangle shape below the head. Make the rear of the body a pointed shape as shown.

3. Put antennae at the head and add an eye. Put stripes on the wings and detail at the end of the body.

4. Add legs with tiny hairs as shown. Carefully erase unwanted lines. Shade your cricket in if desired.

Grasshopper

Just like crickets, the **grasshopper** makes music by rubbing its wings together. Grasshoppers and crickets are part of the same insect family. A grasshopper can jump a distance twenty times the length of its body. Imagine if *you* could jump twenty times the length of *your* body! Grasshoppers can be very harmful to a farmer's crop because they eat many different types of vegetables. Sometimes, grasshoppers will attack a field in a huge noisy swarm that looks like a giant cloud approaching.

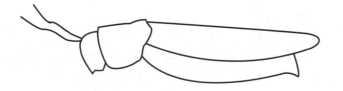

1. Start with a small oval as the head and long, narrow ovals as the body. Sketch in the antennae.

2. Put in lines and detail at the head. Make the underside of the body segmented as shown. Add two flattened wings on the upper part of the body.

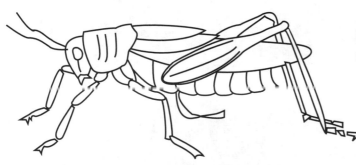

3. Add six jointed legs. Back legs should start in the middle of the body. Erase unwanted lines.

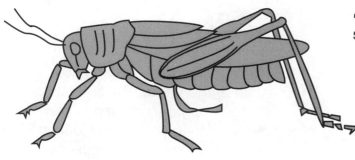

4. If coloring your picture in, use a nice shade of grass green.

Praying Mantis

The **praying mantis** holds its front legs up so it looks like it's praying. These front legs are very strong. The praying mantis uses them to catch other insects and even frogs. A praying mantis is usually green or brown in color. It uses its color and shape to *camouflage* itself, or blend into the branches and leaves of trees. When a praying mantis sits completely still, it looks just like a twig.

1. Start with a triangular-shaped head with two long oval shapes attached as pictured. Blacken the head and part of the two body ovals as shown.

2. Add eyes, facial detail, and two antennae to the head. Put two fat, jointed arms up near the head. Now add two very long and skinny jointed legs to either side of the longest oval. Make the last segment of each leg jagged. Put in light shading and add detail as shown.